One Day, So Many Ways

Lincoln
Children's Books

ALASKA

GREENLAND

CANADA

ICELAND

SCOTLAND

IRELAND

UNITED KINGDOM

FRANC

USA

SPAIN

NORTH AMERICA

MOROCCO

HAWAII

MEXICO

CUBA

JAMAICA

SENEGAL

M

BURK
FAS

ECUADOR

AMAZON PERU

BRAZIL

**SOUTH
AMERICA**

ONE DAY,
SO MANY WAYS...

All around the world, children are going about their
everyday lives. But how they do it is different from place
to place and country to country. We all do things a little
differently—but look closely and you'll see that we have
plenty in common too: we like to be with our friends,
eat delicious food, and play freely, even if our houses,
schools, and games aren't the same. Dive in and see
whose life you'd like to try out, even just for a day!

PATAGONIA

SWEDEN

FINLAND

NMARK

POLAND

RMANY

EUROPE

-Y SERBIA

ISRAEL

EGYPT

AFRICA

TANZANIA

SOUTH AFRICA

RUSSIA

ASIA

MONGOLIA

AFGHANISTAN

NEPAL

BHUTAN

INDIA

JAPAN

CHINA

VIETNAM

INDONESIA

OCEANIA

AUSTRALIA

NEW ZEALAND

ANTARCTICA

EARLY MORNING

The day is just beginning. Homes are different around the world—which one would you like to wake up in?

ZANZIBAR, TANZANIA
This house is built on a beach. The sea salt in the air has made the roof rusty.

NUUK, GREENLAND
Houses here are bright and bold. Set on a hill, this house overlooks fjords, icebergs, and mountains.

CAIRO, EGYPT
In a city-center apartment like this, you're never far away from family. Grandparents, uncles, and aunts all live in the same apartment building.

REYKJAVIK, ICELAND
Houses in Iceland need extra protection from the wind and cold. This one has sheets of blue iron on the outside.

NOVOSIBIRSK, RUSSIA
If you live at the top of an apartment building like this one, you get the best views of the city.

SOWETO, SOUTH AFRICA
Children live together with their parents and grandparents in these small houses.

PARO, BHUTAN

Apartment buildings in this town are brightly colored and overlook a river.

JINING, NORTHEAST CHINA

Houses in this part of China have rooms around the outside and a courtyard in the middle.

THE OUTBACK, CENTRAL AUSTRALIA

This house is part of a sheep farm in the outback. There are no towns for miles.

GALWAY, IRELAND

Living in a town house is fun if you know your neighbors. You can play together in the street.

EQUATORIAL FOREST, ECUADOR

Would you like to wake up to find a monkey on your roof? That's what often happens here!

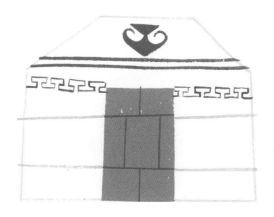

ERDENET, RURAL MONGOLIA

This yurt is a home for nomadic tribes. All the family sleep together in this round tent.

LONDON, ENGLAND

English houses can be really old! This one was built over one hundred years ago. It has roses around the door.

WAKE UP!

The moment when we open our eyes to a new day is something we all share. But where we sleep and what we see, feel, and hear around us is different, depending on where we live.

TOKYO, JAPAN

Hanako is woken up by her brother, Ishi, who has set two alarm clocks for 6:30 a.m.! They turn on the news and get ready to help Okaasan ("Mom" in Japanese) make breakfast.

LOUGA, SENEGAL

As dawn breaks, Kwame wakes to the sound of birds—and the rooster! Kwame shares a bed with his mom. When it's hot, they move a mat outside to sleep.

SAO PAULO, BRAZIL

In the summer, Arami and her brothers and sisters sleep on their porch—in hammocks made from cotton. Arami's bedroom is used to store sacks of food to sell at the family's grocery business.

MELBOURNE, AUSTRALIA
Spencer shares a room with his younger brother. It's hot outside, so their mother sprays their faces with water to wake them.

COPENHAGEN, DENMARK
It's hard for Olli to wake up today. He was dreaming of being a pirate and would rather stay in his dream. But his family's pet cat, Diko, won't let him sleep any longer.

POKHARA, NEPAL
When Bikram wakes, it's very cold outside, and hard to get up! The bed and room he shares with his mother, father, and brother is now empty—they are outside preparing breakfast for the family.

BREAKFAST

The first meal of the day can be something sweet or savory depending on where you live. What do you like eating for breakfast?

PARIS, FRANCE
Julie and Maxime dip their croissants in hot chocolate.

TAIPEI, CHINA
Tina and Chang have fried breadsticks and a cup of warm soybean milk.

HO CHI MINH CITY, VIETNAM
Hieu and Minh slurp pho for breakfast every day. Pho is a meaty soup with rice noodles and spices like ginger, chili, and star anise.

MUMBAI, INDIA
Tanya has idli and sambhar for her breakfast. Idli is a rice cake, and sambhar is a vegetable stew.

MELBOURNE, AUSTRALIA
Liam and Tom eat poached eggs on toast.

MARRAKESH, MOROCCO

Aya's favorite breakfast is pancakes drizzled with honey.

BERLIN, GERMANY

Katharina eats bread, meat, and cheese.

RIO, BRAZIL

Beatriz eats traditional Minas cheese, bread, and papaya.

AMAZON RAIN FOREST, PERU

Every morning, Gina and Luis have tacacho, which is a roasted banana with chorizo sausage. They eat bananas as part of almost every meal.

GOING TO SCHOOL

Around the world, children travel to school in different ways. Some go by car, some go by bike, and some go by bus. How would you like to get to school?

SHETLAND, SCOTLAND
Jimmy and Mhairi wave to seals from the ferry on their way to school.

SEAFORTH, JAMAICA
Sean and Shanice ride the school bus past the beach and palm trees.

TOKYO, JAPAN
Hiroe takes the busy morning train across Tokyo by herself.

CHURCHILL, CANADA
Watch out for polar bears! Walking to school can be dangerous for Nathan and Logan.

LONDON, ENGLAND
Olivia and Ellie join the line for the school bus at the corner of their street.

COPENHAGEN, DENMARK

Sofie and Anna's mom takes them to school in a cargo bike. Sometimes their dog comes, too.

KUMPUR, NEPAL

Mir and Bibek cross the rushing Trishuli River on a rope bridge.

CALIFORNIA, USA

Ava and Randy's mom drives them to school every morning.

NUUK, GREENLAND

Pipaluk rides on the back of her dad's snowmobile.

THE OUTBACK, AUSTRALIA

Bindi and Tak don't go to school because they live too far away. They listen to lessons on the radio.

VENICE, ITALY

Mario and Alessandra take the vaporetto past the palazzos and gondolas.

SCHOOL LIFE

Not every school is the same. In some schools you only go in for half a day; in others you go in six days a week. What is your school like?

HAVANA, CUBA

Hector and his friends wear the Cuban school uniform: red shorts with a white short-sleeved shirt.

SUOMENLINNA ISLAND, FINLAND

Emilia has school lessons at home because not many people live on her island.

WINNIPEG, CANADA

Sarah and Adam go to the same school as their neighbors, in a big old building.

WARSAW, POLAND

Marta and Tomek have to be at school on time. If they are later than 8 o'clock, they can get in trouble.

HANOI, VIETNAM

Linh and Son go to school six days a week, from Monday to Saturday. They study hard for tests every day.

KABUL, AFGHANISTAN

Aamir is seven years old and is going to school for the first time this year. His older brothers go to the same school as him.

BAMAKO, MALI

Some days Youssouf helps his father with his cattle, and other days he goes to school.

GUADALAJARA, MEXICO

Jesus works in the morning, so he only goes to school in the afternoon. Most of his friends do the same.

KINGSTON, JAMAICA

Paul and Julia started going to preschool when they were only two years old. Now that they are both six, they go to kindergarten.

AMAZON RAIN FOREST, PERU

Daniel and Luz go to school by the river, to learn with all the other children from the village.

LEARNING

Sometimes school lessons feel like they go on forever...but other times they just fly by! What's your favorite thing to learn about at school, and whose class would you like to join?

AMAZON RAINFOREST, PERU
Diego and Maria like geography, where they look at maps and learn all about volcanoes and mountains.

RURAL CHINA
Tao and Wing have to learn a lot of facts in their lessons and remember them well.

PARO, BHUTAN
Karma and Adan have a garden at school, where they learn to grow peppers, peanuts, and carrots

BALI, INDONESIA
Budi and Adin learn about conservation in their science class, and how to look after the natural world.

SHETLAND ISLES, SCOTLAND
In her music class, Melissa's learning to play all sorts of instruments, like the fiddle.

TEL AVIV, ISRAEL
Leah likes her Bible study classes, along with art and English.

STOCKHOLM, SWEDEN
Mette likes writing stories about amazing places and characters, and drawing pictures to go with them.

GALWAY, IRELAND
Aoife is really good at handwriting, and has learned to write letters to her pen pal during English class.

PATAGONIA, ARGENTINA
Felipe has a favorite part of math class: when they play their "Math World Cup," using numbers!

CAIRO, EGYPT
Yasmine likes computer science, where she plays a game that teaches her to build an imaginary city.

NUUK, GREENLAND
Ebba learns to speak and write in three languages at school: Danish, Greenlandic, and English.

CAPE TOWN, SOUTH AFRICA
Moshe likes his gym class best. Off the field, he reads about famous sportspeople.

HONOLULU, HAWAII
Mano loves learning about the natural world and how animals live in the wild.

PLAYTIME

Playime is usually the best time of the day. Whose games would you like to play today?

JAKARTA, INDONESIA

Irene and Ahmad play "Elephant, Orange, Ant": the elephant beats the orange, the ant beats the elephant, and the orange beats the ant!

RURAL CHINA

Harmony and Tara sing and play "jump" with a rope they've made from elastic bands.

MUMBAI, INDIA

Krish plays a game called "Horse" with his friends, which involves a lot of running (and chasing people)!

JERUSALEM, ISRAEL

Sometimes Rafael likes to sit quietly and play a counting game with apricot stones.

STOCKHOLM, SWEDEN

Oskar and Ella like a game where they pretend to be scary polar bears playing in the snow.

HAWAII, USA

Iokua and his friends pretend to be surfers in the playground, making sure they don't touch the water and get eaten by sharks!

BARCELONA, SPAIN

Abril and Carla play policemen and thieves with their friends. When the policemen catch the thieves, they all switch sides.

HO CHI MINH, VIETNAM

Tadashi and Pablo play marbles outside their classroom. Tadashi is the best marbles player in the whole school!

HAVANA, CUBA

Ruben and his friends like the playground. He swings on the monkey bars while they climb the castle.

FRIENDS

Every day around the world, friends share time with each other at home or at school. Whose friend would you like to be?

REYKJAVIK, ICELAND
Asta and Jon like to go swimming with their friends after school.

OUAGADOUGOU, BURKINA FASO
Samira and Ismael have lots of friends and are always in a big group at playtime.

MOSCOW, RUSSIA

Maxim is happy playing on his own, but likes to join in lunchtime soccer games.

KATHMANDU, NEPAL

Sunita, Amir, and Bibek are friends—as well as siblings! Sunita is the eldest.

SYDNEY, AUSTRALIA

Rose and Amy grab their towels and meet at the beach after school, where they are learning to swim.

MARRAKESH, MOROCCO

In class, Fatima sits next to her best friend, Rita, who likes to tell her funny jokes.

PARIS, FRANCE

Michelle and Benedicte often have playdates after school. Benedicte has an amazing toy collection.

ANCHORAGE, ALASKA

Ethan and Ryan are in different classes but like to sit together at lunchtime.

KINGSTON, JAMAICA

Tegan and Alwan pass notes to their friends in class.

BARCELONA, SPAIN

Valentina made her best friend, Sofia, a friendship bracelet. Lucky Sofia!

CAPE TOWN, SOUTH AFRICA

Lubanzi and Baraka know most of their friends from church.

QUIET TIMES

Taking time to be quiet and thoughtful can be good for us. What do you think about when you have quiet time?

CALIFORNIA, USA

Kayla and Jacob have yoga class once a week. They have to stretch and balance and be quiet at the same time.

PARO, BHUTAN

When school starts, Yushika and Puran sit still and think with their eyes closed. It's called a morning meditation.

TOKYO, JAPAN

At the end of every day, Ayumi sits quietly and thinks about her day in school, just like all her classmates.

BERLIN, GERMANY

Sophie sits and draws on her own after lunch each day. She is drawing a picture of a cat.

BAMAKO, MALI

Fatim's school is anything but quiet! With lots of children of different ages, it is always lively.

LONDON, ENGLAND
Katie and Rosie have quiet reading time each day in school. They sit on the carpet and flip through the colorful books on the library shelves.

Brandon does not like quiet time! He would much prefer to be running, jumping, shouting, and being silly.

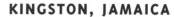

ZANZIBAR, TANZANIA
Mary sits in the small prayer room in her school when she wants some quiet time.

CAIRO, EGYPT
Ali goes to the mosque five times a day with his brothers to pray. It is very quiet.

ANCHORAGE, ALASKA
Austin looks out of the window and thinks about what he is going to have for dinner.

LUNCHTIME

At lunchtime, children around the world eat different foods. What do you eat?

JINING, RURAL CHINA

Lee and Cherry go home to have lunch with their family. Usually they eat rice with pork and vegetables.

NOVOSIBIRSK, RUSSIA

Irina has a three-course lunch every day at school. She has a beetroot soup called borscht to start, then chicken with potatoes. She has a fruit compote to finish.

NEW YORK CITY, USA

Rachel and Sammy sit with their friends in the school cafeteria and eat pizza and salad.

STOCKHOLM, SWEDEN

Johanna and Viktor eat meatballs and fried potatoes with ketchup.

CAIRO, EGYPT

Mido eats Moroccan tagine and couscous.

SHETLAND ISLANDS, SCOTLAND

Lucy and Mhari have fish cakes, potato wedges, and green beans for lunch. Mhari has a dessert of chocolate sponge and custard.

NUUK, GREENLAND

Angelica eats suaasat for lunch, which is a soup made from seal, onion, and potatoes.

TOKYO, JAPAN

Natsumi usually has miso soup with tofu and vegetables, a bottle of milk, a bowl of rice, and some fish.

SUOMENLINNA ISLAND, FINLAND

Veera has lunch at 10:45 a.m. She likes it when boiled potatoes, fish sticks, and salad are on the menu, with milk and crispbread.

WARSAW, POLAND

Klaudia and Wojtek's school lunch is carrot and pumpkin soup with quiche and broccoli.

SUMATRA, INDONESIA

Dewi's favorite part of lunch is the dessert: starfruit, mangosteen, rambutan, and jackfruit.

COPENHAGEN, DENMARK

Maria and Emilie's packed lunches include ryebread, mackerel, cold sliced potato, and some vegetable sticks.

GYM CLASS

All around the world, people like to move! What sports do you like, and what would you like to try?

NOVOSIBIRSK, RUSSIA
Marina practices gymnastics.

RIO DE JANEIRO, BRAZIL
Natalia plays soccer with her brothers.

KATHMANDU, NEPAL
Karuna, Alisha, and Milan play badminton.

MELBOURNE, AUSTRALIA
Ben and Lachlan take swimming lessons at school.

MONTREAL, CANADA
Jordan is a big fan of ice hockey.

SANTA CLARA, ECUADOR
Tatjana and Walter play basketball.

MUMBAI, INDIA
Aishwarya takes Indian dance classes.

VANCOUVER, CANADA
Laurence plays lacrosse.

VENICE, ITALY
Riccardo learns the art of Venetian rowing.

MARRAKESH, MOROCCO
Chaimae likes to skateboard.

BELGRADE, SERBIA
Franko and Helena love to play handball.

HONG KONG, CHINA
Vivian enjoys playing Ping-Pong.

SNACK TIME

Do you like salty or sweet snacks? Or something else?

THE OUTBACK, AUSTRALIA
Jess and Jordan eat Vegemite on toast.

KATHMANDU, NEPAL
Nina and Manish eat vegetable samosas.

TEL AVIV, ISRAEL
Dana eats hummus with pita bread.

PATAGONIA, ARGENTINA
Matias eats an empanada, a stuffed pastry. His is stuffed with cheese.

GUADALAJARA, MEXICO
Elizabeth and Cesar eat mango and papaya.

OTTOWA, CANADA
Audrey and Eric eat maple leaf cookies. Yum!

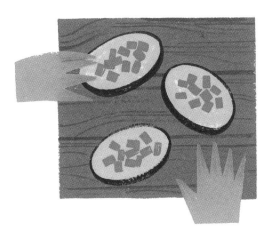

VENICE, ITALY
Giorgia and Daniele eat tomato bruschetta. The bread has olive oil and garlic on it as well as tomatoes.

ANCHORAGE, ALASKA
Tyler and Nick eat salmon jerky. The salmon has been marinated in a yummy sauce and dried out.

BELGRADE, SERBIA
Andrej and Dajana eat yogurt with different kinds of fruit. Today they have blueberries.

REYKJAVIK, ICELAND
Ketil and Hrafn eat dried fish and salt licorice.

PARO, BHUTAN
Kelzang and Dorji eat momo, which are Bhutanese dumplings.

BAMAKO, MALI
Leila eats plantain chips. They are crispy and salty like potato chips!

TIME FOR ART

Now it's time to do something creative.
What would you like to make?

SAN FRANCISCO, USA

Ryan and Austin have to draw pictures of each other. This is called drawing portraits, and you have to sit very still.

AMAZON RAIN FOREST, PERU

Using objects she finds around her, Esther makes rain sticks out of wood, colored string, and tiny stones. When you tip them upside down, the falling stones make a noise like rain.

BARCELONA, SPAIN

Alex takes a walking tour of Barcelona to look at architecture and street art. He likes the bright colors and wavy lines.

NUUK, GREENLAND

Erni's art class has to draw a picture of a tupilak, a kind of magical Greenlandic monster with big teeth.

WAIKIKI BEACH, HAWAII

Anai makes a bracelet from cowrie shells she found on the beach. She threads the twine through the holes in the shells and joins them together.

ROSKILDE, DENMARK

Kristina and Dicte make bowls from clay. First they mold them until they get the right shape. Then they leave them to dry. When they're dry, they can paint them.

AUCKLAND, NEW ZEALAND

Jesse is drawing a picture of his house and his mom and dad for a display at school.

HONG KONG, CHINA

Jin practices traditional Chinese writing with a brush and black ink. He has to work hard to get the shapes exactly right.

DAR ES SALAAM, TANZANIA

Adika and Amri like to make junk models from recycled objects. Today they are making drums out of old coffee cans.

TOULOUSE, FRANCE

Michel makes paper collages. He cuts up bright pieces of tissue paper into squares and arranges them on a piece of paper.

HO CHI MINH CITY, VIETNAM

Vinh and Linh draw pictures of children around the world for a school project.

REYKJAVIK, ICELAND

Jonsi colors a picture of a volcano erupting. He is using yellow for the flames at the top.

HOME TIME

School is over for the day and it's time to go home. How do you get home from school and who picks you up?

FALMOUTH, JAMAICA
Grace and Carleen's grandmother meets them from school. She is always pleased to see them.

TRINIDAD, CUBA
Omara stays in school until 7 p.m. He only has lessons until 4 p.m., and then he can play games and sports for the rest of the time.

HERAT, AFGHANISTAN
Hakim rides home from school on his brother's bike. He balances on the back while his brother pedals.

BARILOCHE, ARGENTINA

Santiago walks home on his own. He only lives down the street from his school.

TAIPEI, CHINA

After a long day at school, Michelle and Tiffany go to another school in the evening to learn to improve their math.

CHICAGO, USA

Kelli and Sam go to an after-school program because their parents work late. They like learning to code.

SHETLAND, SCOTLAND

Craig and Effie skim stones while they wait for a ferry home. They travel with the other children in their class, and their mom meets them on the other side.

CASABLANCA, MOROCCO

Yasmina's school day ends at 5:30 p.m., much later than most countries. She walks home, carrying her books.

YEKATERINBURG, RUSSIA

Vitaly's dad is late to pick him up because of the traffic. It can take a long time to get across the city by car, especially if there is snow.

KARAKORUM, MONGOLIA

Sarangerel leaves school at 3:20 p.m. He walks with his cousins and waves goodbye when they get home.

BRISTOL, ENGLAND

Ava and Louis meet their mom at the school gates. They cycle home together with bike helmets on.

HAMBURG, GERMANY

Clara finishes school at lunchtime. Sometimes she goes home, and other days she stays for school clubs.

AFTER-SCHOOL ACTIVITIES

There is plenty of time left to play after school has finished. What would you like to do?

KOUDOUGOU, BURKINA FASO
Clementine and Thomas feed the family's chickens and goats before their mother will let them play.

CORK, IRELAND
Eimar goes to Cub Scouts once a week after school. Her favorite part of it is camping with her friends.

STELLENBOSCH, SOUTH AFRICA
Jason plays soccer in the street with his friends. His team usually wins.

SURABAYA, INDONESIA
Tri swims in the river with his friends after a hot day at school. He swings from a rope into the deepest part of the water.

LODZ, POLAND
Konstantyn has a piano lesson after school. He has to practice in between lessons to get better.

KYOTO, JAPAN
Aiko is part of a choir. She sings classical music, show tunes, and pop songs with other girls.

TURKU, FINLAND

Otto sits on a riverbank and watches the birds. He likes listening to the water, seeing the boats come and go, and feeding the ducks.

HANGZHOU, CHINA

Bo and Fang spend time with their grandmother after school. They like it when she tells them traditional stories about China.

LUXOR, EGYPT

Isis plays her video game. Her favorite games have superheroes in them.

ADELAIDE, AUSTRALIA

Jenny and Dylan meet their friends and play on the beach after school.

HOMEWORK

No matter where you live in the world, most schools give out homework. Which task would you like to do?

PISA, ITALY
Gabi's homework is to write a fact file of a famous person that she admires.

KOLKATA, INDIA
Raj has to learn a poem to read out loud in class tomorrow.

PARO, BHUTAN
Sonam and Ram are doing a project on recycling and have to collect plastic bottles to take to school.

HALIFAX, CANADA
Jade and Isaac have to interview their grandfather for a history project. He talks to them about what life was like when he was their age.

OTAVALO, ECUADOR

Solange and Will take photographs of all the animals and insects they can find in their yard for a nature project.

TIMBUKTU, MALI

Laurent does his math homework by the light of a flickering kerosene lamp.

TORONTO, CANADA

Ellen and Zoey have to learn to read in French and English—it is hard work!

GOTHENBURG, SWEDEN

Dahlia and Niklas's school does not assign homework. Their teachers think the children work hard enough during the school day.

OAXACA, MEXICO

Marco and Madelena practice their handwriting. They have to copy the same words over and over again and make the letters the same size.

EILAT, ISRAEL

Shoshi does her homework assignments on the computer. She especially likes doing math puzzles.

NOVI SAD, SERBIA

Drasko and Emil have a spelling test tomorrow and have to learn ten words each from a special list.

FAMILY TIME

It's great to spend time together as a family.
What do you like to do with yours?

ROTORUA, NEW ZEALAND
Hannah baking with her grandma.
She likes making chocolate cupcakes
best.

MARSEILLE, FRANCE
Pierre and Madeleine watch TV with their parents. They especially like watching cartoons.

KOPAVOGUR, ICELAND
Tumi spends evenings in the
swimming pool with the rest of
his family. His dad goes in the
hottest pool with his friends,
but Tumi prefers the big pool
with the slide.

KATHMANDU, NEPAL
Raj goes shopping in the market with
his mother. It is always busy, and he
usually sees his friends there too.

HO CHI MINH CITY, VIETNAM
Yen and Van visit the local temple
together. It's a busy place in the evenings,
with sweet-smelling incense in the air.

ANCHORAGE, ALASKA
Juno goes to an ice hockey game with her family. They love it when their team wins!

RIO DE JANEIRO, BRAZIL
Ana Luiza flies a kite with her mom from the rooftop of her house. She can see all the way to the beach from here.

ST. PETERSBURG, RUSSIA
Mischa plays the violin with her mother. Making music together is great fun.

THE OUTBACK, AUSTRALIA
Spencer goes on a bush walk with his dad, looking for animal footprints and watching out for snakes.

DISKO BAY, GREENLAND
Morten goes kayaking in the fjord with his sister. Sometimes they see seals sitting on the rocks nearby.

HELPING OUT

Some children help out with daily tasks at home. Other children just make a mess! Which one do you do?

STUTTGART, GERMANY

Claudia helps pull out weeds in the garden. She has her own vegetable patch where she is growing carrots, too.

GLASGOW, SCOTLAND

Davie and Elspeth have to feed their pet rabbit and clean his hutch once a week.

SAPONÉ, BURKINA FASO

Flora sweeps the courtyard, and Abdoul pumps water from the well. Flora also helps her mother prepare their evening meal.

COPENHAGEN, DENMARK

Carl and Ingrid take the dog for a walk every evening.

STONE TOWN, ZANZIBAR

Amina collects firewood from the beach and forest.

NEW YORK CITY, USA

Julian and Debbie help empty the dishwasher and put their toys away.

MADRID, SPAIN

Eduardo carries the grocery bags in from the car. He puts the food away afterward.

AMAZON RAIN FOREST, PERU

Julio sweeps the floor of his hut and helps his mother and father gather food for dinner.

HONG KONG, CHINA

Raymond makes his own breakfast. If he is asked, he will wash the dishes, too.

NEGRIL, JAMAICA

Selena and Noah water the plants inside the house once a week. They also pick the fruit in the garden when it is ripe.

DINNER

The day is done and everyone heads home for food.
Dinner time is different in every corner of the globe.
What would you like on your plate?

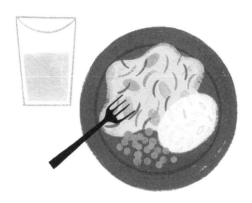

KINGSTON, JAMAICA

Sean's grandmother cooks ackee fruit and
saltfish with rice and peas.

CAIRO, EGYPT

Karim's mom makes great falafel.

MELBOURNE, AUSTRALIA

Jake and Dylan love Greek food—
especially meat souvlaki
with fried potatoes.

BARCELONA, SPAIN

Miriam's family eat paella together in
the evening. She likes the prawns best.

ZANZIBAR, TANZANIA

Joyce, Joseph, and Grace eat street food
from a market stall.

BAMAKO, MALI

Ibrahim sits down with his family to
eat gumbo stew and rice.

ULAANBAATAR, MONGOLIA

Ganzorig's family sit around the fire in their
tent and eat khorkhog, a big meat stew.

WELLINGTON, NEW ZEALAND

Georgia loves it when her dad cooks roast
lamb with vegetables and gravy for dinner
and pavlova for dessert.

SOWETO, SOUTH AFRICA

Junior eats sausages with mealie pap, which is sort of like porridge but is made from sweet corn and vegetables.

HONG KONG, CHINA

For Cherry, instant noodles with vegetables and sliced meat makes a quick and tasty dinner.

MOSCOW, RUSSIA

Artem eats pirog—a big pie stuffed with vegetables and meat.

KABUL, AFGHANISTAN

Kabuli palaw is Mahmood's favorite dinner, which is a mixture of rice and lamb.

BERLIN, GERMANY

Lena's favorite dinner is schnitzel with new potato salad.

HONOLULU, HAWAII

Lani likes having a poke bowl of rice with raw fish, soy sauce, and onions. She loves it when they have pineapple for dessert.

GALWAY, IRELAND

Finn always has fish fingers, chips (or French fries), and peas on Fridays.

TOKYO, JAPAN

Hiroe likes curries, especially chicken katsu curry served with rice.

HAVANA, CUBA

Ernesto enjoys rice and beans for dinner.

READING

Reading is a great way to learn about the world and understand the people in it. What sort of stories do you like?

ACAPULCO, MEXICO

Sofia and Luciana prefer reading books that are about soccer players and real life, instead of fairy tales and folk stories.

JAVA, INDONESIA

Rio's favorite story is about a boy who can transform into a tiger at night. It's a traditional tale from Sumatra.

MUMBAI, INDIA

Vihaan's mom tells him stories about Indian gods with elephant heads and eight arms.

POKHARA, NEPAL

Bishal likes traditional Nepali stories about frogs, sparrows, and kings.

TRINIDAD, CUBA

Mari is learning to read in Spanish. She reads a short book from school with her mom and dad every night.

LONDON, ENGLAND

Harriet reads to herself every night before she goes to bed. Her favorite stories are about fairies and pixies.

THIMPHU, BHUTAN

Kiba loves it when her mom reads her stories. She especially likes stories about other countries.

HELSINKI, FINLAND

Emma loves stories about the Moomins, who are supposed to live in the woodlands of Finland.

WARSAW, POLAND

Martin likes stories about dragons and knights. He imagines that he is a knight saving a princess.

BUENOS AIRES, ARGENTINA

Thiago likes stories about brave children who try their hand at anything and go on adventures.

ESSAOUIRA, MOROCCO

Youssef's grandfather tells him the best stories about magic and mystery, all from his own memory.

STOCKHOLM, SWEDEN

Alice's favorite character is a girl called Pippi Longstocking, who has red hair and is very spunky.

TIME FOR BED

It's bedtime. Children around the world close their curtains and get ready for bed. What do you do before you go to sleep?

FLORENCE, ITALY
Giulia says good night to all her toys before she goes to sleep. Sometimes she tucks them into bed, too.

TORONTO, CANADA
Lea and Sam snuggle up together on the sofa to hear a bedtime story about children like them.

AKUREYRI, ICELAND
Before bed in the summer, Kristin and Egill need to draw their thick curtains because the sun barely sets on some nights.

AARHUS, DENMARK
Isabella and Mads brush their teeth in front of the mirror for two minutes. Their mom makes sure they brush every tooth.

MEXICO CITY, MEXICO
Alejandro tells his worry dolls his problems and put them under his pillow. When he wakes up, the dolls have taken his worries away.

GALAPAGOS ISLANDS, ECUADOR

Darwin has a shower before bed. Even in the evening it is really hot, so a shower is refreshing.

CAPE TOWN, SOUTH AFRICA

Ethan has a snack before he goes to bed. He shares his bedroom with the rest of the family.

BAHIA, BRAZIL

Julia has a glass of milk before she goes to bed, to help her sleep well.

TEL AVIV, ISRAEL

Karmela prays before she goes to bed. She thinks through the things that have happened that day and says thank you.

CHARLOTTETOWN, CANADA

Naomi and Anouk get to stay up late on special occasions, but are usually in bed by 8 p.m.

NOVOSIBIRSK, RUSSIA

Yasha has a bath with bubbles and toys to warm himself up. In winter, it can be so cold that his shampoo freezes in the bottle!

THE HIGHLIGHTS OF MY DAY

Can you remember everything that happened to you today?
Here are some of the best things that happened to these children
around the world.

It rained heavily on the way home from school,
but Bella and Richard didn't mind. They
jumped in the puddles all the way back!

ALTAI, MONGOLIA
Batbayer enjoyed playing with his new puppy after school. He has
little teeth but can't bite very well yet.

EDINBURGH, SCOTLAND
Elspeth and Archie went to their aunt's house for tea.
They built a den in the yard with their cousins.

SYDNEY, AUSTRALIA

Ruby and Isla had their favorite sandwiches in their lunchboxes today—cheese and ham.

SAINT PETERSBURG, RUSSIA

Valeria got to the next level on her computer game and was really happy!

BOSTON, USA

Jimmy and Mark's grandmother called them on Skype to say hello and talk about coming to visit.

FAIRBANKS, ALASKA

Ryan and Mary's dad bought a new snowmobile and let them have a turn on it with him. It went really fast.

AUCKLAND, NEW ZEALAND

Oliver's dad took him for an ice cream down by the harbor after school. They sat on the dock and looked at the boats in the water.

DUBLIN, IRELAND

Aoife was chosen to be part of the school field hockey team. She is looking forward to playing in a match against another school.

HONOLULU, HAWAII

Jason got ten out of ten on his spelling test at school. He's really pleased because he worked very hard for it.

NIGHTTIME

In most places around the world, it is dark at night, but not everybody is in bed. Do any of these things happen at night where you live?

WARSAW, POLAND

Aleksander's father sometimes takes him outside to watch the stars. He points to the different constellations and teaches him their names.

MUMBAI, INDIA

As Tamara sleeps, fireworks go off to celebrate a special occasion, whooshing high into the sky and exploding into a rainbow of colors.

NOVOSIBIRSK, RUSSIA

In wintry Siberia, the snow has started to fall outside Alexei's bedroom window overnight.

VANCOUVER, CANADA

Moths, bats, owls, and coyotes come out at night while Frank and Justin sleep.

HAVANA, CUBA
The sound of music being played in the night drifts into Marisol's room, but doesn't wake her up.

KANDAHAR, AFGHANISTAN
Everything is quiet in Tela's house, apart from the sound of her father gently snoring.

COPENHAGEN, DENMARK
Frans and Jeppe's parents are going out for the night, so a babysitter is looking after them until they get home.

HONG KONG, CHINA
While Yumiko is in bed, the skyscrapers around the center of Hong Kong play a music and light display.

GUADALAJARA, MEXICO
While Jesus is asleep, streetlamps are lit and people walk, talk, drink, and dine until late in Mexico.

DREAMS

When we're sleeping, our minds wander. Sometimes we remember our dreams in the morning but not always. What do you dream of at night?

TOKYO, JAPAN
Haruki dreams that he is in a rocket, blasting off to space, to live with the rabbit on the moon.

WELLINGTON, NEW ZEALAND
Laura dreams about swimming under the ocean like a mermaid. Her hair flows out behind her, and she makes friends with a bright red octopus.

ANCHORAGE, ALASKA

Aurora dreams that she has won the lottery. The first thing she does with her money is buy a castle for her mom.

NEW YORK CITY, USA

Zoie dreams she can fly. She floats into the sky and becomes as small as a bird.

BARCELONA, SPAIN

Hugo dreams that he is invisible and can do whatever he wants all day without anybody finding out.

CALGARY, CANADA

Audrey dreams that she is driving a team of sled dogs along the ice on a snowy day. They go fast over the bumps.

VENICE, ITALY

Francesca dreams Venice has turned into a waterpark. All the rivers are full of warm bubbly water, and there are slides everywhere instead of bridges.

QUITO, ECUADOR

Carlos dreams that he is a monkey dancing on the roof of his school in the rain! His teachers tell him to go away, but he just keeps on dancing.

BAMAKO, MALI

Mariam dreams that she has a brand-new bicycle. She cycles along the river for days and days until she reaches the sea. She has never seen the sea in real life.

WEEKEND FUN

The weekend is finally here! When your school week is over, what do you do for fun?

BELGRADE, SERBIA
Teodora has a picnic in their local park with her friends.

SHETLAND ISLES, SCOTLAND
Isla, Zander, and their mom and dad take a wild and windy walk to a castle.

ANCHORAGE, ALASKA
James and Aurora are having a sleepover at their aunt's house. They are sharing the same bedroom as their cousins.

AMAZON RAIN FOREST, PERU

Weekend days are much like other days in the Amazon, except sometimes there are festivals and celebrations.

HAVANA, CUBA

Silvio watches a game of baseball in the local park. He wants to be a baseball player when he grows up.

REYKJAVIK, ICELAND

Asta goes camping with her dad and his friends. It is a bit uncomfortable sleeping in a tent but she likes it.

RIO DE JANEIRO, BRAZIL

Tania goes to the beach to watch her brother play soccer. She loves walking barefoot on the sand.

TAIPEI, CHINA

Yanting goes to the movies during the weekend. He loves eating popcorn before the film starts.

LONDON, ENGLAND

Fiona and Georgie go to a birthday party. It has a magician, party music, and a cake lit up with candles.

PATAGONIA, ARGENTINA

Benjamin plays in the street with his friends. Sometimes they play tag. Other times they play soccer.

SUMATRA, INDONESIA

Johan and Siska take a trip to the lake to go swimming with their father. It's always nice and warm.

THE OUTBACK, AUSTRALIA

Isabella rides horses across the outback with her dad. It's a great way to explore the land near their house.

WEEKEND JOBS

There is more time at the weekend to help your family and do useful things together. Which of these jobs would you like to help with?

JINING, RURAL CHINA

Lok and Jun help their mother and grandmother harvest rice in the paddy field.

BERLIN, GERMANY

Katarina helps to sort the recycling into paper, glass, and plastic

KABUL, AFGHANISTAN

Nabi helps his dad fix the car. He likes getting greasy oil on his hands, but it can be hard to wash off.

OUAGADOUGOU, BURKINA FASO

Aida works at her mother's market stall during the weekend.

STONE TOWN, ZANZIBAR

Abdullah helps his father untangle fishing nets so he can catch more fish next week.

GALWAY, IRELAND
Siobhan goes to the supermarket with her mom and helps pick out food for the week.

HELSINKI, FINLAND
Emilia helps her mom cook in the evening, and sets the table.

MELBOURNE, AUSTRALIA
Kylie and Jack wash the car and help to polish it.

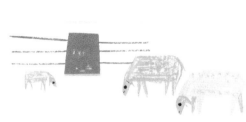

ULAANBAATAR, MONGOLIA
Altan helps to sweep around the yurt and tend to the animals.

GUADALAJARA, MEXICO
Jose Luis helps his mother do the laundry. He gathers all the dirty clothes and takes them to the laundromat.

WELLINGTON, NEW ZEALAND
Maia helps her dad clean out the shed, then take the boxes they don't want to the garbage dump.

MUMBAI, INDIA
Anaya helps her dad paint her bedroom. It is going to be a light shade of pink when it is finished.

LEARN MORE ABOUT THE COUNTRIES IN THIS BOOK...

There are 195 countries in the world today—this is just the tip of the iceberg.
Find out more about these 50 countries in these fact files. Which is the largest?
Which is the smallest? And how many words for "hello" can you remember?

AFGHANISTAN

Continent: Asia
Population: 35.5 million
Languages spoken: Pashto, Dari

Salaam! Afghanistan is a country in the Middle East that gets hardly any rain. Sometimes there are kite-flying competitions where powdered glass is attached to the strings so kite runners can cut the strings of the other kites. The winner is the last kite left flying!

ARGENTINA

Continent: South America
Population: 44.3 million
Languages spoken: Spanish

Buenos días! Argentina is a huge country, the eighth largest in the world. You can find it at the bottom of South America. The most southern part, Patagonia, is the closest bit of land to Antarctica on Earth.

AUSTRALIA

Continent: Oceania
Population: 24.5 million
Languages spoken: English

G'day! Australia is home to some of the deadliest animals on the planet—there are 20 types of venomous snake, plus poisonous spiders, sharks, crocodiles, and box jellyfish. You'd better watch your step!

BHUTAN

Continent: Asia
Population: 800,000
Languages spoken: Dzongkha

Kuzoozangpo La! Bhutan is a Himalayan kingdom with a Buddhist religion. The word "Bhutan" actually means "Land of the Thunder Dragon." The name comes from the dramatic storms that roll into Bhutan from the Himalayas.

BURKINA FASO

Continent: Africa
Population: 19.2 million
Languages spoken: French
Bonjour! Burkina Faso has the largest population of elephants of all the countries in West Africa. Bet you're all ears about that!!

BRAZIL

Continent: South America
Population: 209.3 million
Languages spoken: Portuguese

Oi! Brazil is the fifth largest country in the world, and puts on the largest carnival in the world, the Rio Carnival.

CANADA

Continent: North America
Population: 36.6 million
Languages spoken: English and French

Hello! Canada is famous for its wonderful wildlife. One town, Churchill, is known as "the polar bear capital of the world." Every autumn hundreds of polar bears gather by the town as they journey north.

CUBA

Continent: North America
Population: 11.5 million
Languages spoken: Spanish

Hola! Cuba is an island in the Caribbean, famous for salsa dancing, vintage cars, and beautiful beaches. I bet you didn't know that blowing your nose in public in Cuba is very rude—people do it in private.

CHINA

Continent: Asia
Population: 1.4 billion
Languages spoken: Mandarin Chinese

Ni hao! China is the fourth biggest country in the world and contains big cities as well as rural paddy fields. Every year in China is represented by one of 12 animals, which symbolize the character of people born in that year.

DENMARK

Continent: Europe
Population: 5.7 million
Languages spoken: Danish

Hej! Denmark is a Nordic country, along with Sweden and Norway. It might be small, but it's very good at inventing things. Denmark invented wind energy, the loudspeaker, handball, and Legos!

ECUADOR

Continent: South America
Population: 16.6 million
Languages spoken: Spanish

Hola! You can find both the rain forest and mountains in Ecuador. Did you know that guinea pigs aren't pets in Ecuador? They are food! They taste a bit like rabbit, and are a special dish.

EGYPT

Continent: Africa
Population: 97.6 million
Languages spoken: Arabic

Salaam aleikum! Most of Egypt is covered by the Sahara Desert. The River Nile is the country's major river, and most people live along it or near it.

FINLAND

Continent: Europe
Population: 5.5 million
Languages spoken: Finnish, Swedish

Hei! You can see the northern lights in Finland's Arctic Lapland region. Some people say that Father Christmas lives here. If you go south, you'll find a huge labyrinth of patches of water, so many that Finland has been named "the land of a thousand lakes."

FRANCE

Continent: Europe
Population: 65 million
Languages spoken: French

Bonjour! Did you know: French people eat around 30,000 tons of snails a year, served with garlic, parsley, and butter. Would you like one? France is also famous for its croissants and baguettes.

GERMANY

Continent: Europe
Population: 82.1 million
Languages spoken: German

Hallo! Germany was home to two of the world's most famous musicians—Beethoven and Bach—and many classical concerts are performed today. Its most famous food is wurst, which is a type of sausage.

GREENLAND

Continent: Europe
Population: 56,500
Languages spoken: Greenlandic, Danish

Aluu! Greenland is the world's largest island, measuring 836,000 square miles. However, not that many people live there because almost 80% of it is covered in ice.

ICELAND

Continent: Europe
Population: 323,000
Languages spoken: Icelandic

Goðan dag! Some of Iceland's traditional food seems a bit strange to outsiders: on special occasions, they eat puffin, reindeer, dried fish, cod cheeks, and rotten shark. In the winter, there are only a few hours of daylight each day.

INDIA

Continent: Asia
Population: 1.3 billion
Languages spoken: Hindi, English

Namaste! India is the second most populated country in the world, as over 1.3 billion people live there! There are 22 official languages including Bengali, Hindi, Urdu, and Tamil.

INDONESIA

Continent: Asia
Population: 264 million
Languages spoken: Indonesian

Halo! Indonesia's tropical jungles are home to some of the most exciting animals on the planet, including the Komodo dragon, tiger, orangutan, elephant, and leopard.

IRELAND

Continent: Europe
Population: 4.8 million
Languages spoken: English

Hello! Ireland's old stories include talk of a little fairy called a leprechaun, who is very mischievous and has hidden a pot of gold at the end of a rainbow. It is divided into the Republic of Ireland, in the South, and Northern Ireland, which is part of the United Kingdom.

ISRAEL

Continent: Asia
Population: 8.3 million
Languages spoken: Hebrew, Arabic

Shalom! The beautiful country of Israel includes a lake called the Dead Sea, which is one of the saltiest bodies of water in the world. It is impossible to sink in it, and very easy to float!

ITALY

Continent: Europe
Population: 59.4 million
Languages spoken: Italian

Ciao! Italy is home to the Colosseum and other ancient Roman ruins. It also invented the ice cream cone, the margherita pizza, and the parachute. Fantastico!

JAMAICA

Continent: North America
Population: 2.9 million
Languages spoken: English

Wah gwaan? Jamaica is an island in the Caribbean where people speak English and you can eat jerk chicken, curry goat, and ackee and saltfish. Did you know the world's fastest man, Usain Bolt, comes from Jamaica?

JAPAN

Continent: Asia
Population: 127.5 million
Languages spoken: Japanese

Konnichiwa! Japan is made up of many different islands. Most people live on one of the largest four: Honshu, Hokkaido, Kyushu, and Shikoku. It is good manners to slurp your noodles loudly when eating in Japan—it shows that you are enjoying your food!

MALI

Continent: Africa
Population: 18.5 million
Languages spoken: French

Bonjour! Mali is one of the largest countries in Africa but most people live along the Niger River. In Mali, only two in every five children go to school—fewer than anywhere else in the world.

MEXICO

Continent: South America
Population: 129.2 million
Languages spoken: Spanish

Hola! Mexico borders the south of the USA. Tabasco, Tequila, and Chihuahua are all places in Mexico and have given their names to spicy sauce, a drink, and a breed of tiny dog.

MONGOLIA

Continent: Asia
Population: 3.1 million
Languages spoken: Mongolian

Sain uu! A third of the people who live in Mongolia are nomadic—they move around from place to place depending on the season to find the best conditions for their camels, cattle, and horses.

MOROCCO

Continent: Africa
Population: 35.7 million
Languages spoken: Arabic, Berber

Salaam aleikum! You can find a fortune-teller in nearly every town in Morocco, and a shop in every souk that sells potions, herbs, and elixirs.

NEPAL

Continent: Asia
Population: 29.3 million
Languages spoken: Nepali

Namaste! Mount Everest, the tallest mountain in the world, is in Nepal, along with eight of the world's ten highest mountains. Only about 4,000 people have ever climbed Mount Everest, which is 29,000 feet high.

NEW ZEALAND

Continent: Oceania
Population: 4.7 million
Languages spoken: English, Maori

Kia ora! Did you know there are more sheep in New Zealand than people—27 million at the last count? That makes just under 6 sheep for every person!

PERU

Continent: South America
Population: 32.2 million
Languages spoken: Spanish, Quechua, Aymara, and multiple local languages

Rimaykullayki! More than half of Peru is covered with jungles and rain forest, and people think there may be fifty Amazon tribes in the Amazon rain forest that have never had contact with the outside world.

POLAND

Continent: Europe
Population: 38.2 million
Languages spoken: Polish

Czesc! Poland in Central Europe is home to some of the strongest men in the world— more "World's Strongest Man" winners have been Polish than any other nationality.

RUSSIA

Continent: Europe
Population: 144 million
Languages spoken: Russian

Zdravstvuyte! Russia is the largest country in the world, stretching over eastern Europe and Northern Asia. It spans 11 time zones and includes 180 other ethnic groups as well as Russians.

SCOTLAND

Continent: Europe
Population: 5.4 million
Languages spoken: English, Gaelic, Scots

Guid mornin! Scotland has 790 islands and a mysterious lake called Loch Ness, where a underwater monster is supposed to live. Its most famous musical instrument is the bagpipes.

SERBIA

Continent: Europe
Population: 8.8 million
Languages spoken: Serbian

Zdravo! Serbia has been an independent country since 2006. Did you know Serbia grows a third of the world's raspberries? You've probably eaten one without knowing that it was grown in Serbia!

SENEGAL

Continent: Africa
Population: 15.9 million
Languages spoken: French, Wolof

Na nga def! Senegal is an African country with a hot, tropical climate, and has only two seasons: rainy and dry. It gets its name from the Senegal river, which borders the country to the East and North. In fact, the word "Senegal" means "our boat" in Wolof!

SOUTH AFRICA

Continent: Africa
Population: 56.7 million
Languages spoken: isiZulu, Afrikaans, English, isiXhosa, siSwati, Sesotho, Xitsonga, Sepedi, isiNdebele, Setswana, Tshivenda

Molo! South Africa is rich in gold and diamonds—more of these things come from South Africa than anywhere else. It's also where you can find the black mamba, the fastest snake on the planet.

SPAIN

Continent: Europe
Population: 46.77 million
Languages spoken: Spanish

Hola! Spain is famous for bull fighting, tapas (lots of small dishes that are shared), and flamenco dancing. One of its most famous buildings, the Sagrada Familia in Barcelona, is still being built, over a hundred years after it was started.

SWEDEN

Continent: Europe
Population: 9.9 million
Languages spoken: Swedish

God dag! On Midsummer, in June each year, everyone in Sweden goes to the countryside to celebrate with music, dancing, and special foods like herring and boiled new potatoes.

TANZANIA

Continent: Africa
Population: 57.3 million
Languages spoken: Swahili, English

Jambo! There have been humans living in Tanzania, Africa, for over two million years. Archaeologists have studied bones and tools found in Tanzania to study human evolution. It's also home to elephants, lions, buffalos, and rhinos.

UNITED KINGDOM

Continent: Europe
Population: 66.2 million
Languages spoken: English

Hello! The United Kingdom is made up of England, Scotland, Wales, and Northern Ireland. English people drink more tea than any other country in the world!

USA

Continent: North America
Population: 324.5 million
Languages spoken: English

Hello! The USA is the world's third largest country and has 50 states including New York, Washington, Texas, and California. The highest roller coaster in the world is in Jackson, New Jersey—would you dare to ride it?

VIETNAM

Continent: Asia
Population: 95.5 million
Languages spoken: Vietnamese

Chao ban! Schools in Vietnam start every day with the sound of a gong—not a school bell. It's a great way to start the day!

Inspiring | Educating | Creating | Entertaining

Brimming with creative inspiration, how-to projects, and useful information to enrich your everyday life, Quarto Knows is a favorite destination for those pursuing their interests and passions. Visit our site and dig deeper with our books into your area of interest: Quarto Creates, Quarto Cooks, Quarto Homes, Quarto Lives, Quarto Drives, Quarto Explores, Quarto Gifts, or Quarto Kids.

First published in 2018 by Lincoln Children's Books, an imprint of The Quarto Group.
400 First Avenue North, Suite 400, Minneapolis, MN 55401, USA.
T (612) 344-8100 F (612) 344-8692 **www.QuartoKnows.com**

The illustrations were created in gouache
Set in Triplex

Published by Rachel Williams
Designed by Nicola Price
Edited by Eryl Nash and Katie Cotton
Production by Kate O'Riordan and Jenny Cundill

Manufactured in Slovenia GP082018
9 8 7 6 5 4 3 2 1